Skylark

ENCOUNTERS IN THE WILD

JIM CRUMLEY

ONE

THE SKYLARK IS a particularly good omen in my
life. It is the habit of a lifetime that I harvest particular moments in nature's company, pressed flowers
between pages of memory. They are few and far
between, but I revisit them all often, as I might
revisit favourite records and books.

For example: an otter I got to know at Isle Ornsay
(we talked to each other over dinner – the otter's
dinner); a mute swan pen on Loch Lubnaig (when
she was sick, dying as it turned out, she sought me
out and slept for ten minutes in my shadow); a starry
saxifrage high on Beinn a' Bheithir near Glencoe (I
had accidentally dropped a coin into a rock crevice,
lost the coin but found that single bloom aglow in
its dark, roofless crypt, and I emerged immeasur-
ably richer as a result); two red-throated divers on

a high lochan on Raasay (I watched them in the late evening from my tent, they were the last thing I heard before I fell asleep, the first thing I heard when I awoke); a humpback whale in Glacier Bay, Alaska (it came alongside a small whale-watching boat as I leaned over the gunwhale, its four-inch eyeball made blatant eye-contact while its immense whale brain thought... what?). That kind of thing. But with skylarks it is a bit different. They keep turning up, guardian angels when life is occasionally troublesome, they keep singing me back out of dark days into sunlight, they keep rescuing me and restoring to me a sense of perspective, which the introverting nature of a writing life can occasionally misplace. And the first of all my consciously harvested moments was the first skylark. I would like to say that I remember it as if it were yesterday, but the truth is that I have amassed about sixty years of yesterdays since that particular moment, so something must surely have frayed round the edges by now and something must have gilded my souvenir of it to keep it so vivid. But what I remember is this.

SKYLARK

I was a child with a football, I had gone across the street from the family prefab on the edge of Dundee to the first of the fields of Angus that washed the far side of the street. We – a small cabal of local bairns – had commandeered a strip of the field edge for a football pitch. One touchline was simply the edge of the growing crops, or stubble or ploughed land in season. The farmer could just as easily have ploughed up our pitch, but he never did, and it remained sacrosanct until the bungalow builders moved in and the farms of Backhill and Hillside were obliterated forever. That predestined day, I had obviously expected others to turn up and play but no one did. I ran around practising what would now be called ball skills, but without even a wall to kick the ball against I got fed up and simply sat on the ball, like Oor Wullie on his bucket, and waited for something to turn up. What turned up was larksong.

I cannot imagine now that I knew it was larksong then. If I had, I would not have been so astounded by what happened next, so astounded that it endures undimmed. But I knew it was birdsong. I was a child with a musical ear and a curiosity about nature, and there and then the two fused in one single, spellbinding collision.

A bird stepped up out of the grass, the very square foot of grass I was staring at, distracted and bored. The bird stepped up onto the air, gained a little height, and then it sat on an invisible landing on an invisible stair.

Singing.

It all happened at once – the stepping up, the sitting on the air, the singing. There had been grass and silence. Now there was the bird, the sitting on the air, the singing.

Although I lived in a prefab, I understood stairs and landings. My grandfather lived in a tenement, upstairs, with landings. My primary school had stairs and landings. The idea that the bird climbed by way of an airy staircase and paused on its landings was there from the beginning. Blackbirds, sparrows, chaffinches, robins, gulls, geese, flew through my life from one place to another, usually in straight lines. This singing bird did not fly that way, it *rose*. It climbed and it paused, it climbed and it paused, it climbed and it paused, and the only way I knew how to do that was with a staircase and landings.

It climbed towards the sun. I seem to remember shading my eyes with one hand as I watched it climb, singing as it climbed. Even when it reached a landing and sat there, it still sang. And then it climbed again. It climbed until its stair went right through its roof, and now there was nothing between it and the sun. But still it climbed and still it sang. Then it reached some kind of perch in the blue and sunlit air and sat there, rocking on its wings, singing, and then the notes of the song fell to earth and they were warm snow that landed all around me, gathered in piles and then in drifts, and changed my life and my view of the world at once and forever.

I remember now – as I try to reassemble the child's unknowing vision through the twin prisms of the man's years and knowing – that the bird paused finally in the eye of the sun so that I could not look at it. But I could still hear it, and as the sound of it was so much more miraculous than the look of it, I could not feel short-changed, what with the sunlight and the song and the warm snow.

Then the bird was out of the eye of the sun again and back in plain sight, and it was clear at once that it was coming back downstairs. Then it seemed to lose control, for it bounced down from landing to landing, missing out all the stairs in between. Suddenly it was back in my portion of the world and the grass came back into view, suddenly the bird stopped singing, suddenly it fell. There was a sound, the softest of soft thuds, as if a twig had fallen on a cushion of moss. I can hear it as clearly now as I heard it then, but mercifully without the lurch of stomach and the flutter of heart that was my original response. Then there was just an absence, an absence of bird, song, stair, landing, warm snow. It seemed wrong that the sun still shone.

The bird had hit the ground not ten yards away. I ran to the spot. I expected smithereens of feather, bone, blood. Instead there was nothing. No bird. But then something moved beyond a tussock, something awkward and broken. There was the bird, trailing the tip of one fanned-out wing along the ground. I ran to it. I would help it, gather it up, take it home, save it. I had no idea how.

But then it flew.

I stopped.

I remember something like utter helplessness. I stared after it until it vanished in the grass again. And that was the moment a part of my heart was lost to nature forever.

I know now that the descending, singing, male skylark controls the last few feet of flight after the song stops, in order to effect a soft landing; that the broken-winged one was a different bird, the female, the nest-sitter, luring me away from the nest by feigning a broken wing, the oldest trick in nature's book. But I never learned to stop marvelling at the first of all my skylarks.

◎ ◎ ◎

The child of six became the man who writes about nature for a living. In a rare dalliance with fiction I wrote a short novel based on the life of my other grandfather, a professional footballer in Dundee in the early years of the twentieth century, and hardly the terrain of the nature writer. Until, that is, skylarks infiltrated the story unbidden and uninvited, and became a motif of hope and triumph over adversity for him. I lent his childhood self the story of my first skylark and it grew from there, to a First World War battlefield, and I even put the words of Hoagy Carmichael's immortal song *Skylark* on his lips to console his old age. I gave him a dream of the trenches that haunted him all his life after the war to end wars, but which always ended with a skylark when the guns fell silent.

And then, as if to put a seal of blessing on the endeavour, and while I was still writing the novel, I was ambushed by Richard Strauss and Kiri Te Kanawa.

I had the radio on in the kitchen. I was cleaning up; drying dishes, I think. A voice announced Strauss's *Four Last Songs*. I have known the work for many years through a recording my mother used to play sung by Elisabeth Schwarzkopf. It had always defined the work for me, but it had never got the better of my emotions. But it was Kiri Te Kanawa whose voice came on the radio and I heard the work as I had never heard it before, and it moved me to tears where I stood with a dishtowel and a plate in my hand. I went into town the following day and bought the CD.

It was a simple coincidence. I was writing the book, I played the music. They were entirely unconnected events. But as I worked on the detail of the book I began to study the detail of the music. The *Four Last Songs* were Strauss's last compositions, written after a silence of many years. He died in his eighties, not long after he finished them. So it seemed logical that they might have a message to impart. He was signing off. I started to concentrate on the last of the *Four Last Songs*, and then on the end of that last song, the final utterance of the final utterance, the last syllables of epitaph. Strauss gave them not to the human voice at all, but to the simplest of orchestrations. There is no tempo, no melody. The last note of the voice had been conspicuously understated, cushioned on an unresolved chord. Then the orchestra moved towards the slowest, softest of conclusions, a kind of contented weariness. There was a simple, drawn-out major chord in which bass tones predominated. But scattered through it, like stars on a moonless night, were the short intrusions of two flutes, again and again and again and again, and these are Richard Strauss's last utterance. What was their message?

The first three of the *Four Last Songs* are settings of poems by Herman Hesse. The fourth, *Im Abendrot* ("At Dusk"), is by Joseph von Eichendorff. The poet evokes the end of a journey through a quiet landscape of encircling valleys, which is also the end of life's journey. But even as the sky begins to darken, even as the poet contemplates the possibility of death, two larks climb into the still air.

The flutes are skylarks! There is that last sung line, that last inconclusive sung note, the orchestral weariness, but then, unconcerned with death and sure of themselves and their living and their singing, there are the skylarks. The boy who lives on within me cannot forget the first of all my skylarks. The writer I became put that first skylark into the life of the grandfather I never knew. I donated an episode of my life to his. Then the radio played me Kiri Te Kanawa. Skylarks have turned my head forever.

◉ ◉ ◉

SKYLARK

When I began writing this *Encounters in the Wild* series in 2014 and met Carry Akroyd, whose artwork graces all its covers, she introduced me to the poetry of John Clare (1793–1864). Her own book, *Nature's Powers and Spells* (Langford Press, 2009), has the subtitle of *Landscape Change, John Clare and Me*, and in it she explains and demonstrates through her own artwork how Clare influenced her art. She wrote of him that "his eye, mind and heart reach across time through his writing". I thought about that for a while (it is the handsomest of compliments), for there are any number of great poets who do not reach across time, but rather they simply hold a mirror to their own time for us to gaze into. What convinced me that Carry was right was a passage from his poem, *The Skylark*.

First of all he invokes not the bird but the brown hare in a green field of young corn:

Where squats the hare to terrors wide awake
Like some brown clod the harrow failed to break

And in the course of writing another title in this *Encounters* series, called *Hare*, how often did I focus the glasses in the skylark-rich fields of the Carse of Stirling on what proved to be not a brown hare but one more brown clod the harrows failed to break? So at once Clare's image claimed timelessness to itself.

But it was when he introduced the skylark into the poem – *a dust spot in the sunny skies* – that he really reached out and touched this twenty-first-century kindred spirit, for the glimpse he offers is one framed by the mindset of boys in a field at the very end of the eighteenth century as the bird topples to earth and makes for its nest (we now know he wrongly ascribed the high singing flight to the female, but what the hell – it's poetry, not biological theory):

> *Where boys unheeding past – ne'er dreaming then*
> *That birds which flew so high would drop again*
> *To nests upon the ground where anything*
> *May come at to destroy. Had they the wing*
> *Like such a bird, themselves would be too proud*
> *And build on nothing but a passing cloud,*

SKYLARK

As free from danger as the heavens are free
From pain and toil – there would they build and be
And sail about the world to scenes unheard
Of and unseen – O were they bird,
So think they while they listen to its song,
And smile and fancy and so pass along
While its low nest moist with the dews of morn
Lies safely with the leveret in the corn.

That boyhood view could so easily have been my own, had my pals come out to play football that day, but instead they left me alone to grapple with a miracle of nature that has sustained me ever since. To have your poetry reach new ears two hundred years after you wrote it, and to have it ring so truly in those new ears, is a kind of immortality, as immortal as larksong. So thank you, Carry, and thank you John Clare for further illuminating an Encounter in the Wild that I thought for sixty years was mine alone.

TWO

THE ISLAND OF PABBAY is among the most unsung of all the Hebrides. No one ever wrote a Pabbay Boat Song or a Pabbay Bridal Song, or if someone ever did the songs are sunk without trace. The island lies between Mingulay to the south and Sandray to the north, and towards the southern end of the Western Isles. It is not to be confused with Pabbay off the west coast of Harris, Pabay Mor off the west coast of Lewis, or Pabay to the north of Broadford Bay off the east coast of Skye; and not to mention Orkney's tendency to contract Papa Westray to Papay, or Papa Stour in Shetland.

The Pabbay in question has nothing in common with these others except that they are almost all small, unprepossessing and unsung (delectable Papa Stour is the arguable exception to all of the above), and they probably all accommodated a priest or priests or a monk or monks, for the name

in its various spellings is an old Norse word for
Priest Island or Monk Island. Hold that thought
while I digress a little.

There is little in the physical appearance or the
history of Pabbay to commend it to the wider world.
It has been uninhabited for more than a hundred
years; a single standing cottage offers mute, inglo-
rious testimony to the island's lost era, as does a
Pictish stone into which a cross has been carved by
a later, cruder hand than the original Pictish artist.
The human population can only have numbered
dozens at its zenith.

Sailors do tend to sail on by. Pabbay has no
anchorage to speak of, and not so much a landing
stage as occasionally negotiable rocks. As a result,
those same sailors miss out on two of Pabbay's
noteworthy characteristics. One is that it is girt
with sea cliffs that offer spectacularly challenging
"routes" for rock climbers with a screw loose. (I
slipped the quotation marks round "routes" for
my own peace of mind, for none of the definitions
of the word that I comprehend bears the slightest
resemblance to that rarefied interpretation.) But

the other noteworthy characteristic is that Pabbay is symphonic with skylarks.

How do I know, and what persuaded me ashore there to camp for four nights when so many have sailed on by? It was a few years ago now, but the sound of the symphony is undulled. It came about through an old friend, David Craig – a writer of rare distinction, Britain's first professor of creative writing, and a fine rock climber. He wrote to me one day: he had signed on with a party of rock climbers to visit the sea cliffs of Pabbay and Mingulay. A boat would ferry them from Barra to Pabbay, thence to Mingulay four days later, then back to Barra five days after that. Barra is reached by ferry from Oban. One of the party had pulled out. Did I want his place?

David knew well that I am no rock climber, and equally well that I have a healthy addiction to islands and island wildlife. He would climb some days and join me for the others. He thought I might enjoy it. I thought so too. At two weeks' notice I cleared a nine-day space in my diary. And so I jumped ashore from a sea that was almost flat calm, and turned to catch my pack and tent as they were thrown after me.

The boat's engine diminished into silence and we looked around, my friend and I and seven or eight strangers, and walked the short distance to the only obvious camping spot. As I unsheathed my tent and spread it out on the island machair, my ears, my head, my heart, my every sensibility, filled up with the raised voices of a choir of skylarks. Welcome to Pabbay.

While the climbers climbed, I wandered the island, swam in the ocean, watched the wildlife (this included three calling corncrakes and what sounded like thousands of snipe), wondered over the old stone souvenirs of Pabbay's lost civilisations (these included a Celtic monastery – it really was a monks' island), but more often than not I could be found hanging out with the skylarks.

Three-quarters of Pabbay is standard-issue Hebridean rock and bog and machair. But the fourth quarter is where the skylarks live. The explanation is as eccentric as its consequences are remarkable. Sometime in the late nineteenth century, the Atlantic hurled a sandstorm at that end of the island. The sand smothered it right over its 300-feet-high crest, and there, after the storm passed on, it lay. And there, well over a hundred years later, it still lies. When we say an island is "uninhabited" we mean uninhabited by people, and uninhabited by people is almost always good news for nature. Nature looked at the transformed fourth quarter of Pabbay and its complete absence of people, and saw an opportunity.

How long after the sandblow had passed did it take before the first marram grass appeared there? And how long after the marram grass before the first primroses? And how long after the marram grass and the primroses before the first skylarks? And where did they come from and how did they know? I have no idea. But my ignorance of such matters does not trouble me, for I am content that nature knows how to do these things, that its every instinct is dedicated to the relentless exploitation of opportunity, however large or small, however isolated or integrated, however ancient or utterly new. It is quite possible that there were sparse populations of skylarks and primroses elsewhere on Pabbay before the sand came, and that these provided the colonists.

The appropriate word for this eastern quarter of the island is that increasingly rare and precious condition of nature in our own time – profusion. That first day I set foot on it, just as May nudged into June, it was not possible to climb its slopes without treading on flowers at every step. Yet the chief glory of the place was not that barely credible breaking wave of pale yellow, but the skylarks.

I found twenty nests no great distance apart without crossing the ridge, and I could easily have missed five times that number. Yet my presence in their midst barely seemed to register with the birds, so unaccustomed were they to people (mostly they *do* sail on by) that they had never learned to fear them. It occurs to me now (and only now, for sometimes I am a little slow to register such details) that not once did I see the "broken wing" ruse that is the skylark's routine whenever danger threatens a nest.

There is another possible explanation for the skylarks' fearlessness. I had been on the island for two days before I could pinpoint the source of a faint unease that had been nibbling away at the nature writer's basic instincts. There were so many ground-nesting birds, yet there was so little sight or sound of alarm. Awareness crept over me with the kind of caution that stems from the fact that I was something of a fish out of water. Then the explana-tion: there were no predators. The only mammals were a handful of scruffy sheep, and grey seals on the low-tide rocks. There were no hawks, no falcons, and the big black-backed gulls and the eagles were much more attracted to Mingulay's conurbations of rabbits. The combination of this state of affairs and the sandblow had created on Pabbay a skylark paradise.

What was true of skylarks in their primrose-strewn quarter was just as true of snipe over the rest of the island. They drummed and tick-tocked in their hundreds from dusk till dawn, and (because of their fearlessness) from dawn till dusk. All the snipe of my previous acquaintance in all the snipey airts of Scotland have drummed high overhead. On Pabbay they drummed low overhead. So even as the corncrakes grated out the most intolerably unsociable non-stop, all-night-long, clockwork dirge, drumming snipe buzzed the domes and ridges of the tents while their tick-tocking kin amassed a hideous backdrop of a thousand out-of-synch metronomes. Sleep in such an avian madhouse was a more distant prospect than St Kilda.

The din subsided with the sunrise, which was about 4a.m., at which point I would realise that the skylarks were up. So I bathed in the sea to try to counter the effects of sleeplessness, crossed the island to the foot of the skylark slopes, and hung out with the skylarks. I got myself stoned on lark-song before breakfast.

◉ ◉ ◉

A kind of timelessness kicked in. The sheer volume of so many open throats was exquisitely stupefying. I have truly no idea how many skylark pairs graced that sunrise, but if I had been assured by someone who knows how to count birds on such a scale (and cares enough to want to) that there were more than a hundred it would not have surprised me. Instead,

I *was* surprised – astounded – by the cumulative effect, a throbbing abstraction of larksong in which no individual's song was discernible from any of the others, so that I wondered idly what Sibelius would have made of it, for his has always been the voice of northern landscapes in my ears. I can no longer remember whether or not that sunrise pitch of larksong was sustained through all daylight hours. Did it fall silent for a few hours around noon? And if so, is it possible that a passing sailor who decided to drop anchor and row ashore for a picnic lunch might sail away again oblivious to the routine miracle hidden deep in the marram grass and the primroses, because his visit coincided with skylark siesta?

When I did finally stir myself and wander back to the tent for breakfast, it was usually much later than I thought, and half a morning had crept by, so deeply had I given myself up to the wonder. The little routines with which we all mark time in our workaday lives have little meaning on uninhabited islands, and you learn quickly to do without them. Such places are otherwise aligned, for time is annihilated.

Having written that last sentence down just as you see it on the page, I wondered at once why it sounded vaguely familiar to me. It is a particular satisfaction of my job that from time to time I trip over moments of insightful coincidence in the writing of my distant predecessors. The John Clare example is perhaps not a surprising one, but sometimes the moments spring from unlikelier sources. One such is J.M. Barrie.

I am an admirer of Barrie's prose writing, and among the cluster of novels there are also a few pieces of non-fiction that reveal aspects of the character of the man, and in at least one instance, his voice.

In May 1922, Barrie delivered the rectorial address at St Andrews University, on the theme of "Courage". The speech was subsequently published and I stumbled across it in a bookshop in St Andrews. Remember I asked you to hold the thought about Pabbay meaning Priest Island or Monk Island? At one point in *Courage* he talks about his friend Captain Scott of the Antarctic. Then there is this:

How comely a thing is affliction borne cheerfully, which is not beyond the reach of the humblest of us. What is beauty? It is these hard-bitten men singing courage to you from their tent; it is the waves of their island home crooning of their deeds to you who are to follow them. Sometimes beauty boils over and then spirits are abroad. Ages may pass as we look or listen, for time is annihilated. There is a very old legend told to me by Nansen the explorer – I like well to be in the company of explorers – the legend of a monk who had wandered into the fields and a lark began to sing. He had never heard a lark before, and he stood there entranced until the bird and its song had become part of the heavens. Then he went back to the monastery and found there a doorkeeper whom he did not know and who did not know him. Other monks came, and they were all strangers to him. He told them he was Father Anselm, but that was no help. Finally they looked through the books of the monastery, and these revealed that there had been a Father Anselm there a hundred or more years before. Time had been blotted out while he listened to the lark.

That, I suppose, was a case of beauty boiling over, or a soul boiling over; perhaps the same thing. Then spirits walk.

⊙ ⊙ ⊙

SKYLARK

The boat came down from Barra after four days. We passed our tents and packs on board and followed them. Pabbay dwindled and we headed south for Mingulay. The engine thudded across the open water. It is said of the island of Papa Stour in Shetland that in summer mists the local boats could navigate safely there because the scent of its teeming wildflowers carried far over the sea. Likewise, they might have found Pabbay because of the sound of its larksong.

THREE

WEST OF THE DAYLIGHT MOON

Just west of the daylight moon and hard on the heels
of the shroud of a departing thundercloud,
a skylark reintroduced the thunder-dumbstruck land
to singing.
Then lark after lark they rose and their songs
fell to earth as flakes of ringing silver
that cracked a smile on the stone-deaf frown
of Beethoven.

His inner ear stirred, and his quill hand
crossed page after page, for the larks
had reintroduced him to singing
and symphony.
And the darkness of deafness turned and fled
just as the thundercloud had roared then yielded
to the silent but more glorious furies of rainbow
and larksong.

SKYLARK

THE ARCHITECT OF SONG

Blue, sang a skylark,
and singing, drew
a blue column of song.

Song column! thought a hawk,
and thinking, knew
there was a lark on top.

Red, drew a talon,
and drawing, slew
the architect of song.

Silence, found a skylark,
and finding, chose blue
and song

and began to draw
the column anew
on the field's red-smudged page.

ENCOUNTERS IN THE WILD

THE SKYLARK THAT SANG
AT THE TOMB OF THE EAGLES

The skylark that sang
at the Tomb of the Eagles

chiselled upwards a thin column
of runes, primitive truths

bound up in catchy slurs
and jazzy triplets, like Bechet

on a ground of deep blues.
So it was when tomb-builders

made landfall at Isbister,
found biddable stone to chisel

runes and truths of their own,
and set aside a portion of headland

and the next eight hundred years
to memorialise the passage of their days

SKYLARK

across the face of the island
and domed them in an unlettered grave.

The eagle's shrill anthem
was the struck harp of their song,

and talon and bone they honoured them
as they honoured their own.

Aarkum the Bard squinted skywards
under his raised hand

towards the rising improvising lark
and mouthed two prescient syllables:

"Besh-ay", Song Island.
Skylark, eagle, builder, tomb –

it is all the same song.
It is all the same unfinished song.

FOUR

ONE OF THE MOST LIKEABLE traits of high summer is warm winds; unhampered warm winds down from the mountains that command low, rounded, summer-grassy hillsides to sway to their restless rhythms. On the north and north-west-facing slopes of the Ochil Hills above Sheriffmuir, a little to the north of Stirling on an afternoon of late June, such a wind is at work on such a hillside, furrowing that broad brow as it cruises among tall grasses and heathery tussocks and clusters of bog cotton, creasing the hill's open face with laughter lines, opening and closing sudden mouths in the grass with every gust. In such a wind, the ancient hillside stillness of this corner of the massif is youthfully animated and sunlit green.

And this is a skylark hillside, and this is a skylark wind. The particular demands of skylark flight are surely never so effortlessly simple as they are on such a day on such a hillside and in such a wind. Watch this one poised on a tussock, a brown study of fish-scale patterns in orderly rows, the tail garnished with giveaway stripes of white edging, the crest up-curved to a smooth point. The bird awaits a signal from the wind, a thumbs-up, an urging gust. Lift-off is gently inclined and silent. The transformations from gentle incline to vertical columnar flight, and from silence to song, coincide within a few airborne seconds, a few feet of ascent. The song is full-throated from the first note, as self-confident as the opening bars of Beethoven's *Fifth* or Armstrong's *West End Blues*. There is no preamble, no subtle dropped hint of the glories to come. The glories start with the downbeat.

The flight is a blur of wingbeats that swat the air, every stroke specifically engineered to produce vertical lift rather than forward momentum. It cannot be a technique unique to skylarks among all the birds of the air, but in the skylark it is uniquely deployed. On a hillside like this one where there are many skylark nests, there are also many low-level flights during which the fliers look much like other small brown birds on the wing. But the skylark deliberately selects a strikingly different flight technique for the vertical climb, and for which sustained song is apparently essential; either that or it is the other way round, and the flight technique is essential to project the song. It is not designed to climb in easy spirals like a sparrowhawk, or to power-climb like a golden eagle, or to streak up in erratic, tilted, hunting diagonals like a swift with its mouth open, a turbo-charged flytrap. Instead, the skylark climbs backwards, or at least back-first, and inch-by-inch, and all the while shedding shards of song. The speed of the climb is somehow slower than you think should be the outcome of such energetically deployed wings.

Larksong and larkflight are, of course, tools of biology and evolution, and have been for who knows how many millennia, but for a handful of centuries they have also been the raw materials of poetry.

Norman MacCaig, for example, in *Landscape and I*:

That sprinkling lark jerked upward in the blue…

"Sprinkling" is inspired. The lark climbing above me in the Ochils sprinkled the hillside with discarded notes. And yes, that arguably un-poetic "jerked" is a spot-on observation of the nature of the rising flight.

George Mackay Brown, for example, in *A Child's Calendar*:

A lark splurges in Galilees of sky…

Who but such a poet with such an ear and such an eye for nature's particular Orcadian cadences would bracket "lark" and "splurges" side by side in the same line? But as I climbed the hillside and lark after lark rose ahead of and behind me, and to left and right of me, such a proliferation of extravagant gestures, such ostentation as a means of announcing territorial rights and ambition, is a living breathing definition of the verb "to splurge", yet it took a great poet to wed it to such circumstances as these. And:

…what peltings of song!

He wrote that about skylarks too (in *Following a Lark*), for that drenching downpour of larksong en masse when "sprinkling" is just too genteel for what falls to earth.

Because this land slopes away below them as soon as they take off, and because this particular wind washes down from the north-west and meets this particular hillside head-on and curves uphill as it does so, generating thermals, and because the wind is warm, then a skylark lifts from this of all hillsides on this of all days and in this of all winds with thistledown ease.

◉   ◉   ◉

Some song columns are taller than others, some songs last longer than others. I am happy to assert that no one on earth knows why a particular skylark limits the height of a particular column or the duration of a particular song. (Timing unbroken spells of larksong is an old game among their human admirers, and by common consent the average is somewhere between two and three minutes, but there have been extravagant claims of up to half an hour.) Guessing why is easy, but actually knowing why is elusive for non-skylarks. I could speculate that what with the nature of this hillside and the warmth and direction of the wind, the relative ease of lift-off and staying buoyantly aloft, all that would be conducive to tall song columns and correspondingly long songs, but the evidence of my own eyes and ears from a seat on a flat rock near the hilltop suggested otherwise.

For over an hour I watched and listened for every new outbreak of song, and followed as many rising birds as possible in my binoculars. I was surprised by how many flights lasted no more than about half a minute, much of which was spent in a restless, twitching hover not more than a hundred feet above the ground. My singularly unscientific methodology (as befits a singular un-scientist) took no notes, compiled no data and no report and reached no conclusions. Except this: the skylarks which did climb much higher and whose songs were correspondingly longer, seemed to me to be a small minority of all the birds that rose singing. Perhaps these and these alone were the singing males with nests and mates on eggs or with chicks to feed and necessarily staking some kind of territorial claim, and the others – the low fliers with the shorter songs – were young birds flexing their wing-and-song muscles. Or perhaps it was the other way round. Or perhaps every singer was staking a territorial claim and some were just more flamboyant than others?

All of which sounds infinitely more prosaic than this:

Hail to thee blithe Spirit!
Bird thou never wert,
That from Heaven, or near it,
Pourest thy full heart
In profuse strains of unpremeditated art.

Percy Bysshe Shelley (1792–1822), the crown prince of skylark poets, certainly knew the value of a belter of an opening verse with which to beat his readers about the head. His *To a Skylark* layers imagery as thickly as semi-quavers in a climbing yard of larksong. And it is arguably both churlish and a bit picky to challenge his ardour and his palette with a sliver of doubt, and so challenge posterity's acclaim of the poem, even if I am pretty sure I spent longer accumulating that doubt than he did listening to his single skylark – if indeed a single skylark is what he heard. Heard, please note, not saw:

In the broad daylight
Thou art, unseen, but yet I hear thy shrill delight.

He cannot see his skylark! So how sure can he be that he is hearing only one? I have very good eyesight and very good binoculars, but in one hilltop hour of concentrated watching and listening I realised that often the song of one skylark was replaced or at least overlapped by the new song of another, closer to me or lower in the sky and therefore louder. Strauss knew about overlapping larksongs, hence two flutes rather than one. But Shelley gave no clue that the possibility had occurred to him. It is possible, of course, that there was only one skylark singing and that he heard the song from beginning to end, but he did not tell us that he listened to the whole song. The skylark was still singing when his poem ended with a plea that surely still resonates with any nature poets who were ever stopped in their wandering tracks by a singing skylark:

Teach me half the gladness
That thy brain must know,
Such harmonious madness
From my lips would flow.
The world should listen then – as I am listening now.

◉ ◉ ◉

I too am listening now, but the song has changed, or rather the nature of the song has changed, and I have begun to think that the purpose of the song has also changed. It reaches my ear in short snatches of a few seconds at a time, and with a hint of urgency which I may, or may not, be imagining. And whenever it stops I hear other larks further off, higher up. Then the urgent song kicks in again and drowns them out.

SKYLARK

What's going on? Anyone who has tried to pinpoint a lark in the air from the wavering nature of the sound knows the difficulty.

Where is it?

Higher? Much higher?

Lower? How much lower?

I cannot remember having encountered this kind of larksong before, and I confess to being briefly baffled. Then all is revealed.

I have been looking much, much too high. Even a dozen feet off the ground was too high. Even eye-level was too high. The bird, now that I have found it, is standing on a tussock not ten yards away and it is very definitely watching me. My first response is to wonder how long it has been there, how long it has been trying to attract my attention away from all its airborne kin. No one ever wrote a poem about a skylark on the ground. Every few seconds it sings for a few seconds, stops singing, stares at me through the one black eye I can see, then sings again, and this little rhythmic ritual goes on and on. In the pauses between bursts of song, all the other singing birds of the hillside drift in

and out of earshot, so that I hear them adrift, unfo-
cussed. Then the song from the tussock snaps back
in and re-establishes a focal point. Shelley never
heard this.

The bird seems edgy. It takes longer than it should
for me to realise what is going on. I'm too close.
This bird has a nest nearby and the place where I
chose to sit (thinking I was on the periphery of the
hill's nesting territories) is too close to it, at least for
the bird's comfort. So he sings not *to* me but *at* me
in a way that is different from all the other singers,
because the purpose of this bird's song is to attract
and hold my attention, and (I suspect) to convey to
his mate and all the other skylarks within earshot
that I am here and my presence is troublesome.

And then it dawns on me that this is the singing
bird's variation on the theme of the broken wing
trick. No sooner does the thought register than he
flies a few yards across the hillside, stands on another
tussock, and repeats the process. So I rise to my feet
and I move conspicuously away from him, so that
he knows I am leaving. He flies again, perches again,
sings again. Go, good riddance, he sings.

So I raise a hand to him, turn my back and walk away across the hilltop and some distance down the other side before I sit down again to think about what I have just seen.

◉ ◉ ◉

Beyond the hilltop the landscape transforms. Instead of fields, foothills and mountains slung under a limitless curve of sky, the south-facing slope is locked into a green bowl of overlapping hillsides as introverting as the north-facing slope is liberating. The sky here is reduced to a low-slung roof; the hills rear up abruptly and scrape against the ceiling. And there is no wind. And there are no skylarks at all.

In the sudden quiet, the sudden absence of song, a flickering flame of bright white light grabs at my eyes from lower down the slope. Over a few minutes I see that it is not so much a flame as a winding parade of white sparks low above the hill-side grass, and edging showily eastwards and gently uphill. It is a column of butterflies on the march. They are large whites, the most copious of our butterflies whose numbers are swollen every year by migration from Europe. You find them stowing away everywhere, from your back garden to absolutely anywhere else in the land. But on that green summer hillside where the loudest sounds are the drip and trickle of a dozen hill burns skinny enough to step over (and sometimes overgrown enough to stumble in), they are as exotic as a migration of monarchs.

Their general direction leads across the broad arch of the hilltop at its lowest point and out into the wider world beyond. Have they sought out this side of the hill for a respite from that wider world's troublesome winds? They climb the hill in a kind of steady stutter that more or less holds its course while indulging countless deviations by groups and solitary fliers, but these always return to the main body of the procession. In this way, they take about twenty minutes to cover the quarter of a mile to the skyline. I wonder about their destination. Then I wonder if they know or care.

Some years they produce three different generations, while skylarks may produce three broods of the same generation. The third generation of large whites overwinters here as pupas. The skylarks just abandon the hills for the winter and wander off to the coast. It seems almost certain that from time to time, and wherever their winter wanderings take them, skylarks will eat the pupas of the large whites.

FIVE

A HEAD-HIGH, ice-cold eiderdown of dawn mist lay on the fields, imposing on them a second landscape all its own, as if a silent grey glacier had taken possession of the place. It had been that way for three midwinter weeks, the mist moving in overnight and lingering through every morning. All moving water from Lowland drainpipes to Highland cataracts was sluggish at best, and most of it had stopped moving altogether. The two great rivers that drain the centre of the land and flow east, the Tay and the Forth, urged clumsy, misshapen wads of ice towards the distant sea. Then one day of early February, the barometer twitched tinily towards "change".

Far down the Northumberland coast on the low-tide no-man's-land that swirls and swithers between England and Lindisfarne, a fidgety little eddy of awareness came to rest where a battalion of barrel-chested brent geese flat-footed it over a hundred yards of mud to the mainland shore, and where their arrival seemed to disturb a small cluster of unremarkably brownish birds. These lifted a few feet into the air and flew a dozen yards, muttering tetchily to each other. But when they landed again on top of a small grassy mound the sunlight caught them. Even an apparently oblivious head-down dog walker paused and looked up, and saw their perfectly erect crests and heard a sudden chuckling perkiness course through the flock. Then, in a moment they were gone, a loose arrowhead of thirty birds that had just fired itself north.

Meanwhile, in the high and shivering, misted-in fields between the upper valleys of Forth and Tay and between Lowland and Highland Scotland, the barometer twitched again towards "set fair". For improbable as it seemed right then, right there, the skylarks were coming.

◉ ◉ ◉

The high fields climbed from east and west and from north and south, the highest forming an airy plateau bisected by an old stone wall that had seen

better days. It still served to demarcate the two
highest fields but only because it had a new fence
and a fragmented hedge of uncertain vintage for
company. That threefold barrier was further embel-
lished on both sides by a wide and uncut grass verge,
so that from field edge to field edge was a distance
of three or four yards. There were faint hints of a
track along the verge immediately to the west of
the wall, just enough hints to suggest that feet had
walked this way, perhaps not often and certainly
not recently, but still it wore an air of antiquity.
Occasionally a half-buried and broken flagstone
squinted palely at the sun through long strands of
grass. Furthermore, there was a small feature in a
roadside wall that bounded both fields to the south,
a feature too insignificant and overgrown to be
discernible from a car, but if you happened on it
walking you would surely give it a second glance. A
gap had been purposely let into the top half of the
wall, a gap floored with a flat step that invited you
to pass through the wall into the field.

The reason why you might want to, and for that
matter the reason why I was prowling the roadside

in hopeful search of just such an easy way into the field... that reason broke the skyline on the very crest of the field two hundred yards away: a trio of standing stones, one taller and more erect than the other two, which were more squat and with a pronounced southwards cast. One of the stones wore an oystercatcher the way a clan chief's bonnet wears an eagle feather.

The oystercatchers had also caught this late February wind of change in the weather, this seminal shift in the slow march of the seasons. A week ago they were gathered in numbers down on the low ground, wresting what sustenance they could glean from the frozen farmland and the water's-edge mud of the slower reaches of the Upper Forth where it unspooled a series of loops – the Windings – through the flat farmlands of the Carse of Stirling.

They too were up from the coast, but a week or more ahead of the skylarks. They had worked their way inland via the firth, lingering over the mussel beds at Cramond on the north edge of Edinburgh, the mudflats at Grangemouth, and on past Stirling to these calmer reaches of the Forth where ice cracked thinly under their feet on the riverbanks. Then, when the change came, or when they sensed it was about to come, some scattered inland and uphill, and this one ended up perched on a standing stone, with one of the best views in all the country of the Highland Edge.

The skylarks followed along much the same journey. Some years they arrived in mid-February and their first attempts at song would put a spring in your step despite the fact that the thermometer still said "winter". Some years they had still only made it as far as the Carse by the end of the month, and there they waited, waited for winter to loosen its grip up here. But this long, cold February had stopped them in their tracks in Northumberland. So they waited longer, well served by the ancient knowledge ingrained among the countless tribes of nature that adhere to many different variations on the theme of migration.

Then finally the change came. They grew restless. They were ready. Then the brent geese stomped in among them by the landward end of the Lindisfarne causeway, and the familiar rituals of time and shoreline and transition fell into place. The journey home moved from landmark to landmark, and in two days they had reached the inland end of the Firth of Forth where the river narrowed and began to coil and tighten, and the great rock of Stirling Castle briefly darkened its passage. Here the flock split, the older birds remembering the ways of former migrations across the cusp of winter and spring. One group dipped towards the rock shadows, heading for sunlit fields beyond, where some found their old nesting haunts among brown hares and curlews and lapwings; their fellow travellers pushed on, keeping the company of the river as far west as Flanders Moss, a raised bog where the first meadow pipits were already at work, and where the first redstarts would catch their eye in another month, newly arrived from Africa.

The rest of the skylark flock that had assembled on Lindisfarne now edged closer to the south-facing ramparts of the Ochil Hills, then curved northwards around the western end of the range where the hills relented into the wide spaces of

Sheriffmuir. There they made for one particular hillside, low and rounded and grassy and facing the mountains in the north-west. But this group also had their west-farers and these settled, not on the hillside but on an airy plateau among high fields two or three miles to the west, where a remembered stone stood tall and identified the landscape for them.

So a loose grouping of skylarks that had been variously gathered in by the north wind at the end of last autumn, and found winter respite on the shores of Lindisfarne, was returned to, and united with, its various singing lands. One day of early March I heard the year's first spring song in the field below the stones. By June, there were two singers in the field, three more in the field behind my back, and a sixth that rose near the road with what looked like a substantial dragonfly larva in its mouth, yet it still contrived to sing. But it levelled out at about twenty feet, traversed halfway across the field, curved back to earth, and landed in the thick grass and in silence. From there, it was a short walk to the nest. The purpose of the walk is to fool watching eyes into thinking the nest is where the bird lands, but it never is.

This much I learned from that very first nest of my childhood. By an outrageous fluke I found that first nest with its four warm eggs, and thereafter I watched it and watched over it, for I had decided that without my dutiful presence, all would be lost. So I saw the chicks hatch (I had never seen anything so ugly), fatten and grow, and then one day they were gone. I felt abandoned and unconsulted. I was unprepared for an empty nest.

Football had yielded to cricket in the field edge as summer advanced. Then one day I thought about the nest for the first time in weeks and wondered if I could still find it in the grown crops. I did find it, and it had three new eggs, and the whole miraculous ritual began again.

◉ ◉ ◉

It became clear that the standing stones were central to the oystercatchers' territory. Their nest is a bit of an insult compared to the skylark's neat cup of woven grasses lined with hair or occasionally feathers or scraps of fur, sometimes all three. The oystercatcher hollows out a token scrape in the ground and that's it. The sitting bird surrounds it with an equally notional boundary fashioned from whatever she can reach where she sits. Her mate adopts a watching post nearby, a conspicuous rock, a fallen log, a wall, whatever. The most bizarre choice I have seen was the bonnet of a burned-out car. So in the nationwide inventory of oystercatcher lookout posts, this trinity of standing stones is a kind of royalty.

Once, a skylark perched on the smallest of the stones while the oystercatcher was on the tallest. The roused ire of an oystercatcher on the nesting ground is a thing to behold. It fears nothing and no one (it will stand up to a sheep, a cow, a horse, a tractor). There was a lull of a few seconds after the skylark perched while the oystercatcher took in the full import of such outlandish effrontery. When its first salvo of vocal abuse produced no response, it launched a flat-out, eye-level, black-and-white-and-day-glo-orange attack. It is not too hard to imagine how that must look to a skylark from five yards away, knowing it is the source of the aggressor's discontent. This one had seen it all before. It simply dived down into the grass and vanished, with a second to spare before the oystercatcher landed on the precise spot where it had perched, wings held high, and screeching high-octane outrage. Five minutes later it was back on the very topmost edge of the tallest stone, standing one-footed, and with its head facing its tail, its beak laid flat along its back and covered by its folded wings. But its eyes never stopped working.

Directly overhead, and about a hundred feet up, a skylark sang. And sang. And sang.

AFTERWORD

The skylark (*Alauda arvensis*) is one of eight species of
lark. It has eleven subspecies of its own that range
across Europe and Asia. Britain and France consti-
tute the western extremity of its breeding range.
It will breed on open ground anywhere from sea
coast dunes to mountain summits, but the breeding
density decreases with altitude. Coastal marshes are
the most prolific terrain. In Scotland, it nests from
Shetland to the high Cairngorms to the Mull of
Galloway.

Migration is generally fairly localised – south
into the north of England, or from the heart of the
mainland to the coast. Occasionally they form large
winter flocks of several thousand, notably on the
east and south-west coasts.

The skylark population is declining all over
northern and western Europe. In Britain as a whole,
the population halved in the 1990s, and it still

declines. Changes in farming patterns are thought to be the main cause of the decline. The absence of stubble fields because of autumn-and-winter-sown crops are certainly a factor, and food sources have been affected by insecticides and weedkillers. The skylark appears on the IUCN's Red List of species under threat.

Given how popular the skylark is in the hearts and minds of so many people, it should be comparatively easy to win support – and therefore funding – to do something about that. Demonstration projects, particularly by the RSPB, have shown encouraging results. Even small areas left unsown in fields with winter cereals can make a difference. Management techniques on some of their own reserves have been more than encouraging. For example, the Scottish Ornithologists' Club's two-volume *The Birds of Scotland* (SOC, 2007) notes that breeding pairs at Vane Farm near Kinross rose from thirty-one to seventy-three in just six breeding seasons from 1998 to 2003.

I have already touched on poetry's love affair with the skylark (see Chapter Four), but the sheer weight of numbers of skylark poems surely puts it in a league of its own. Apart from Shelley (twice), John Clare, George Mackay Brown and Norman MacCaig, whom I have already mentioned, the roll-call also includes Wordsworth (twice), Gerard Manley Hopkins (twice), Isaac Rosenberg, C. Day Lewis, George Meredith, James Hogg, Christina Rossetti, Goethe and Ted Hughes. Thomas Hardy also wrote a poem about one of Shelley's two skylark poems (the famous one), so technically you could say that was a skylark poem poem. Hopkins used to visit his grandfather's house in Croydon, as a result of which there is now a pub near the house called The Skylark.

And then there was Shakespeare, who was forever invoking skylarks in some symbolic role or other, notably in *Romeo and Juliet*, who have a conversation in Juliet's bedchamber (or perhaps just her bed) about whether the bird they can hear is a nightingale or a skylark. If it is a nightingale all is well and Romeo can linger a little longer; if it's a skylark then it's time he got his skates on, and his clothes, of course.

SKYLARK

Wordsworth may well have had the scene in mind when, in *To a Skylark*, he wrote:

Leave to the Nightingale her shady wood,
A privacy of glorious light is thine...

In his poem *Skylarks* Ted Hughes was, reliably, more unsentimental than most. His skylark had:

A whippet head, barbed like a hunting arrow...

Ah, but if you are of a squeamish nature, you would do well to look away now. The European Union licenses the shooting and trapping of skylarks. Countries where the concept is enthusiastically pursued include France, Italy, Spain and Greece. Why kill a skylark? Why, to eat it of course. We used to do it here too. The Victorians used cunning little mirrors to lure the larks to the guns. A thousand birds in a day was not an unusual bag, but we seem to have lost the taste for it. And I know it's easy to criticise other countries for their peculiar habits and tastes, but after all, we shoot grouse and manipulate huge areas of the countryside to maximise the number that are available to shoot; and snipe, and woodcock, and we breed pheasants by the million for the express purpose of shooting them. But somehow, shooting skylarks seems so much more crude, so much more a betrayal of our cultural instincts, and of our poetry. After all, whoever wrote a poem about a grouse?

JIM CRUMLEY IS A NATURE WRITER, journalist, poet, and passionate advocate for our wildlife and wild places. He is the author of more than thirty books, and is a newspaper and magazine columnist and an occasional broadcaster on both BBC radio and television.

He has written companions to this volume on the barn owl, fox, hare, swan and badger, and there are further ENCOUNTERS IN THE WILD titles planned. He has also written in depth on topics as diverse as beavers, eagles, wolves, whales, native woods, mountains and species reintroductions, as well as *The Nature of Autumn*.

Published by Saraband
Suite 202, 98 Woodlands Road
Glasgow, G3 6HB
www.saraband.net

ISBN: 9781910192634

Printed in the EU on sustainably sourced paper.
Cover illustration: © Carry Akroyd